A Thousand Little Things:
One-line Poems to Spark a Thought

Ty Gardner

Copyright © 2021 by Ty Gardner

Cover art copyright © 2021 by Shelly Gardner

All rights reserved. No part of this publication may be reproduced, stored in a retrieval system, or transmitted in any form or by any means, electronic, mechanical, photocopying, recording, or otherwise without written permission of the copyright owner except for the use of quotations in a book review.

For more information, address: gardnty@gmail.com

ISBN: 9798594133402

Bury me in words I've penned. I've loved them all, each one a friend. What better way to bid adieu than stay my bones in lines I knew. So pack them tight, each rhyme and phrase, to comfort me in astral days. And if my thoughts do run askew, how apropos my retinue.

Table of Contents

Poems	Page #
1-100	8-17
101-200	18-27
201-300	28-37
301-400	38-47
401-500	48-57
501-600	58-67
601-700	68-77
701-800	78-87
801-900	88-97
901-1000	98-107
Acknowledgments	109
About the Author	111

1. Dry lips in need of wetting.

2. Rustled-leaves scattered by whispering winds.

3. Closed eyes to a warm sun.

4. Feeling things to feel a thing.

5. Gray tunes and paintless rooms.

6. Loving hating the way you hate that you can't love someone.

7. Cool grass and shifting clouds.

8. Red rocks peeking through winter blankets.

9. Daydreaming a rainstorm.

10. The weight of words at the end of your life.

11.   Finger trails through fogged glass.

12.   Cigarette ends in rolling thunder darkness.

13.   Misty autumn architecture and coffee.

14.   The feeling of stars on bare skin.

15.   Whiskey and ash and pulpit stories of loved ones past.

16.   The smell of wrecked childhood in cheap booze.

17.   Salted winds in seaside sunsets.

18.   Peppermint tongues and cream soda Sundays.

19.   First crushes and mood song heartache.

20.   Rolling sweat of frosty Cola in summer swell.

21. Small hands, large sunflowers.

22. Memoirs from gran's life over cider.

23. The idea of love and being in it.

24. Dreaming of falling and waking up.

25. The moon on your back, lips on your lover.

26. A heartbeat pulse like flickering lights.

27. Simple gestures between strangers.

28. Careless youth floating lazily through narrow canals.

29. The great tragedy of the sun's love for the moon.

30. Acrostic crossroads resounding our station throughout the infinite cosmos.

31.   The iron badge of empathy forged in fire.

32.   Drowning in thoughts, and writing yourself a life raft.

33.   Summer days twisted up in contortionist love.

34.   Life, but as a run-on sentence.

35.   A troop of triple moons and fantastical fictitious feasts in treetop forts.

36.   Buttered-jelly scones in noon tea revelry.

37.   A marvel of moonbeam beauty, umber-eyed and lithe as a willow tree whip-crack.

38.   White lies and sugarcoated candy carelessness.

39.   Smiling at life eyes and sobbing at death breath.

40.   Rock bed river bottom thoughts, and sediment feelings.

41.   A hundred hold-me-nows, ink-spattered on cream-colored cardstock.

42.   The weight of loss, and the relief in letting go.

43.   Kissing with a rapture mouth and setting your spirit free.

44.   Days of wind and snow, cold as embittered tongues.

45.   Hookah spiced nightclub rhythms.

46.   Glacial lake runoff to soothe your July soul.

47.   Ice cream kisses in an apple pie love affair.

48.   Temples against backdrops of purple wisteria.

49.   Footing her country road curves for that star-spell smile.

50.   Being the receiver end of telephone love.

51.   Regretting regretting.

52.   Knowing that toast can never be bread again.

53.   The fluorescence of gas station streetlights on rain-dewed roses.

54.   Backstroke daydreams in tempered saltwater taffy.

55.   Forgiving your teenage mother.

56.   Penny candy currency on the childhood stock exchange.

57.   Anything, the way granddad used to make it.

58.   The splendor in a thousand little things.

59.   Living long enough to dislike everything.

60.   The way cool hose water hits August tongues.

61. The first look into the last set of eyes.

62. Ripple love that breaks with the tide.

63. Raving and ranting in Poe-prosed poetry.

64. Pretty as a mink stole, like porcelain-pale perfection.

65. Finding yourself adrift a monsoon mind of melancholy.

66. Enemies of the sun: salty-skinned things that crisp and trim in its heat.

67. Yellow residue on wallpaper from years of tobacco smoke.

68. Turnstile romances that go round and round.

69. Waiting on a turn to wait your turn.

70. All the hoarder talk of hanging on to feelings.

71.   Wandering deep enough into your thoughts and losing your mind.

72.   The soft-tap overtures of September rains on a tin roof time signature.

73.   Watching from the shadows of an ember-orange glow.

74.   Pastures of eye-popping pastels and ivory-crowned princes.

75.   Off-key and singing all the big sads.

76.   White-squalled waves whetted with wrath and wild as a dragon fire deluge.

77.   A company of linen-clothed cherubs–trumpeteers in good tidings of great joy.

78.   Sicilian-smile skies above a whisper of wordless wishes.

79.   The glory of a golden-flowered sun on rolling seas.

80.   Marauders masquerading in people skin.

81. Bathtub cigarettes and Bukowski.

82. The sparkle of snowdrift street lit sidewalks.

83. For the sake of saying we've said a thing.

84. Chroma-soft smile reflections.

85. The halcyon of yester-dreams and never-things.

86. Reaching through the cosmos and grasping a hand.

87. Smiling at smiling.

88. Echos of hearty laughs and unspoken dreams.

89. Arrested daydream developments in follicle-grays.

90. The hum of distant trains masked by low-hanging fog.

91.   Draining the bank to buy love, and going heart-broke.

92.   Finding out that the more things change, the more they stay the same.

93.   Skeleton chimneys in open prairie—brick and stone masonry crumbling 'way to seas of dry tallgrass.

94.   Silent film scenes screaming to thundering piano overtures.

95.   A clearing, deep, in midnight wood.

96.   The majesty of a blood sun.

97.   The salt of things, like wind-whipped waves in winters on Montauk.

98.   Campfire silhouettes.

99.   The crash and crush of ocean hands.

100.   Making dollar moves, hoping things will change.

101. Shadowed-things that drift, like ghosts, in dreams at night.

102. Scabbed knees and hopscotch and raising the steaks when you've got beef.

103. Marionette mouth lines of puppets for love.

104. Sun-bleached and rain-rusted abandon.

105. The thought of thoughts of days gone by.

106. Hearts that beat as thunderclaps.

107. Taking the long way home.

108. The dust of who we were settled in the echoed sentiments of history.

109. The plight of hopeless romantics.

110. The innocence of a whirlwind word romance—pursuits in clicks and finger taps.

111.   Excused betrayal spoken in the flat notes of an accordion.

112.   Speaking through your center brain with nothing left of the r ght thing to say.

113.   Being mindful of coal-hearted lovers and their fiery glow waiting to be stoked anew.

114.   The ashen skies of cities razed.

115.   Flying high on wings of words.

116.   The songless curiosity of birds at a funeral.

117.   An unbiased sun.

118.   High seas hogwash of maritime miracles and sand beach salvation.

119.   Baggage stuff in boxes boxed up like ceiling-high baggage forts.

120.   A dream, reoccurring.

121.	November air that smarts the cheeks.

122.	Heartbreak heartache as a superpower.

123.	Cocaine poetry and chasing that perfect line.

124.	Tucking and folding your treasures safely in an origami heart.

125.	A midnight moon lark.

126.	Patron saints of lotus field oceans.

127.	Parchment parcels of stained-ink vexations.

128.	Taking a leap with pavement feet.

129.	Nomads from no lands.

130.	The craft and charm of a fragmenting glass spiderweb.

131.   Being painfully aware of the pressed-shirt existence you slip your necktie noose around.

132.   Shadows of silhouetting-pines in ember dusk.

133.   Wingless hearts that seek to fly but nose-dive to the ground.

134.   Taking offense at how a person takes offense.

135.   The one the bad dream bogies warned you about.

136.   The shadow shadows hide behind.

137.   A devil in a daisy dress.

138.   The dubious nature of rust.

139.   Biting and biding your tongue in time.

140.   In desert, dark, on open roads.

141.   Hauntingly seraphic dreams of moonlit lavender fields.

142.   The Devil we muse.

143.   Setting free your ghosts on city streets as cotton in the wind.

144.   The gumption to take your place among the stars.

145.   Laying down your bourgeois bones in barren field of midday swelter.

146.   Ocean waves and coming up to breathe.

147.   The beauty of raindrops on caskets.

148.   The great bank of the earth collecting our borrowed carbon debt.

149.   Songs of the cosmos in night sky seas.

150.   Cicada melodies on noon high rivers.

151. Velvet winds that speak in stardust elixir.

152. Honeybee poems of a lemonade laze.

153. Fireside verses of restless whitecap currents.

154. The scattering of stationary seagulls.

155. Relishing the flavor of tongues.

156. The way snow quiets.

157. The burn of tears on slapped cheeks.

158. The way flowers bloom without a sound.

159. Overthinking your worries.

160. How the sun shines, no matter its mood.

161.   Same people, different bodies.

162.   Knowing that no response is still a response.

163.   Waxing lyrical with notes that drip.

164.   Moonshine through Pine tree twilight.

165.   The delicate blush of morningtide dew.

166.   The grief of pale bones under desert suns.

167.   Marks of dusk on whiskey lips.

168.   Caricatures of powder burn on basement light bulbs.

169.   Tinsel sparkle memories from your childhood.

170.   Porch swing downpours.

171. Floorboard vibrations in folk song refrains.

172. Millennium vistas that haunt a lullaby.

173. Solace in dreams of rivers shallow and scattered humanity.

174. A chalice of salt and dissolve and peppered-sentences.

175. Pillars of reminiscence in pond frost.

176. The loneliness of drifting smog.

177. Branches that drip crystalline in springshine.

178. The grace of gliding ballerinas.

179. Oceans folding over harbor towns.

180. December dalliances misting over porcelain evergreens.

181.   Shades of wild moon that gleam river trout.

182.   Sentimental fingers grazing in pastures of desire.

183.   Amaranthine incense and silk sheet serenity.

184.   Silhouettes of early risers in asphalt sunrise.

185.   Subtle salvation in a musical rebirthing of the soul.

186.   The satisfaction of private mementos in passing gaze.

187.   The solitude of river paths to steady the burdened mind.

188.   Comforts of ivory fog from your balcony.

189.   Starshine in a metropolitan power outage.

190.   Night terrors colliding the shores of lighthouse bedrock.

191.   Books with no names in the midnight oil.

192.   Wheatfield symphonies as a mood.

193.   The passive insistence of an April evening deluge.

194.   A drunkard's faith in the bottom of a bottle.

195.   Lingering expectations and the letdown.

196.   Portraits of intimacy in orchards of silver horizon.

197.   The radiant language of winter roses.

198.   Blooming streetlights flickering aloft the neon reflected sidewalks.

199.   Eternity in poems and passages and paintings that sing a wind chime euphony.

200.   Detours into ambrosia meadows and the seclusion of lonely roads.

201.   Displaced scars and wondering who you were back then.

202.   Driftwood delusions and coming to in pine-wet tents.

203.   Alabaster lush seascapes from the sanctity of windless cliffsides.

204.   A velvet wilderness, aching like an avalanche to spill over and smolder you in crimson.

205.   Landscapes of jagged stained-glass bouquets.

206.   Chasing down a coal train of youthful witticisms and hitching a ride back to innocence.

207.   The shudder of something remembered, better forgotten.

208.   Skip and skim of winged-divers in waters glassed by untouched hands.

209.   The sorrow crows know with the changing colors of leaves.

210.   Tapestries of presumptive cosmos uncloaking your shadowed-depths.

211.   Gravestone embraces and reckoning your grievances.

212.   Flushed sweet of cinnamon kisses in October exhales.

213.   Thickets of bramble to hide and hold your tangled brevity.

214.   Faded blooms and tattered edges of bookmarked daisies.

215.   Lakeside crooning in mist and hovering willow.

216.   Seasons wronged by the detriment of daylight savings.

217.   Growing apart, and coming together.

218.   Digging deep to unearth yourself.

219.   Venn diagram courtship and sharing someone's circle.

220.   Making love like you're young again.

221.   Conjuring coffee and books and culminating happiness.

222.   Heaven exposed in the peaking rays of parting cumulus.

223.   Dusting shelves and track marks of your treasured tomes.

224.   Atmospheres of coral and orange blaze and stolen kisses.

225.   Drunken dusk down cobblestone streets in foreign lands.

226.   The spread of evening, jelly-red against the ember burn of the western sun.

227.   Sawdust carpet over wooden plank and scents of milled wood.

228.   Smoke's tongue on fire's lips.

229.   The edge of woods where marsh and trees tilt and lean.

230.   The warmth of knowing arms.

231. Hands that toil and knead in dough of clay.

232. Comforts of blackened-brick from chimney soot.

233. Daring to dare.

234. Measuring life in heaps of coffee filters.

235. Twinkling moments of greatness.

236. Salt-capped pavement and the scorch of slush melt in your boots.

237. The frequency of sighs in middle-age.

238. Sprouts of buried language.

239. Unswallowed voids that roll along in starless nights.

240. Soil-strong hands that caress and tender.

241. The squish of moss and loam between curious toes.

242. The savory of exchanged exhalations.

243. Submissiveness of flocking shadows to the steeple fingers of first light.

244. Floral wallpaper and the stink of unfamiliar cities abuzz outside your hotel room.

245. Cruising through slosh and storm in a borrowed beater and weeping your life's laments.

246. Winter's diagnosis of a cold summer.

247. Madmen ambling in wild abandon, preaching of a time before scratchy beards and lunacy.

248. Abstracts of realism hanging in small-town cafés.

249. The relief of parched throats coated in umber and froth.

250. The lost art of birds gossiping on telephone wires.

251.   Coming back to dog-eared Dickinson.

252.   Summers' lapsing to the exhaustible drone of winter tides.

253.   The course and tug of seas withdrawing.

254.   Dandelion fingers splaying in a western breeze.

255.   Distilled twilight drawing through blind dusk.

256.   Folded hands, the flotsam of living, and the jetsam of self-worth.

257.   Whims of forests wild, and the liberation of being lost in God's backcountry.

258.   Weeping eyes of empty vessels swapping tragedies with screaming shadows.

259.   Loving with your eyes in sentimental quietude.

260.   Death before the bloom.

261. The beautiful madness in dancing naked through desert windstorms.

262. God with a tall glass of something long-fermented stepping over the Bowery bums.

263. Ravines ablaze in blistering black, jittery legs scampering.

264. Conversations with sand-swept skulls in desert broil.

265. Windowpane flies gathering to buzz and rattle their intellect against the glass.

266. Subway rails and the curiosity of compacted strangers.

267. Soft poots across harmonica holes in late-night honky-tonks.

268. Thistle itch on sage scratch.

269. Wandering railways over the plush and sprout of Siberian greenery.

270. Ginsberg and the beatnik gang.

271.   Hay-scatter on highways of dust and brush and static of rural Americana.

272.   Flitting songs of waves, green and tall, busking in towns near the beach.

273.   Rose promises to replace affection in marriages long overdue.

274.   Gutter poets who clink loose change stanzas in tin cups.

275.   Southbound on a gypsy breeze.

276.   Truck stops in towns where weeded-nettle stroll about with no plans for the future.

277.   Worn denim and combat boot combinations.

278.   The tinnitus of poet voices long deceased ringing in your ears.

279.   Buttering your illusion bread with reason and common sense.

280.   The bloat of underbelly society in pale morning rays.

281.   Pre-dawn television static and fathers who fall asleep drinking.

282.   Contemplating the other side of an overpass.

283.   Hailing taxi cabs for the post bar fly confessional.

284.   Outrunning the police that one time.

285.   Wasted youth and sapient minds sacrificed to senility.

286.   Catnap afternoons in dog day drear.

287.   The swoop of buzzards over blistered asphalt.

288.   Sagas of silence from lands of waste and squander.

289.   Giving your density to meadows and dirt for prosperity's sake.

290.   Ruins of castles abandoned to time and shards of broken glass.

291.   Lightning that cackles and bellows beautiful violence.

292.   Dreamless sleep and the stick of muggy summer air.

293.   The duality of being your best and worst self.

294.   The anticipated purge of carnal lust and the space of realized mediocrity.

295.   The strength of men in streaks of tears.

296.   Speaking with hands and fidget eyes in infant courting.

297.   The soft punch of sugar melt.

298.   A space between lightning and thunder that startles the nerves of Fir trees.

299.   A laze of shaded retreat where death confers with his notes.

300.   Wrinkled maps with jotted notes of all your best-laid plans.

301.   The fuss of wind in your hair on days with the top pulled back.

302.   A place where sweetgrass and spring surplus overflow,
       and the insipid gloom of winter lulls.

303.   The hark of roaming roads that ramble 'longside charred remains
       of your childhood home.

304.   Hands and curves.

305.   Drunken ruckus songs on lawn chair Sundays.

306.   Strawberry field harvest sunups in sleepy mountain towns.

307.   Back door breakouts and bike rides through the sapling trees of your youth.

308.   Overcast and ashen outlines heavy as your heartsick.

309.   The crackle and pop of kindling at eventide.

310.   Cupped hands and conversations with newborns.

311.   Pleading spiritedly kaleidoscope dreams of undulating bodies.

312.   A place of dust and campfire smoke, where all the pretty horses roam.

313.   Course words on jilted ears.

314.   Marooned in the soft space of a new dawn.

315.   Cotton clutter clouds of June.

316.   The tall shadow of things to come.

317.   The spirit of a life lived in dying hands.

318.   Dismissing your fears.

319.   Filmstrip flashbacks of bygones.

320.   Musing microcosmic hyperbole in the still of cement handprints.

321.   Parcels of past regrets in dusty dresser drawers.

322.   Spattered vitriol in heated exchanges.

323.   Marinating your wilt in Pinot whites.

324.   The melody of our May rain remorse.

325.   Fog-washed highways and the taillight ghosts that wander them in the dark.

326.   The frostbite fervor of a jerked-thumb on a Midwest daybreak interstate.

327.   Planting your seeds in sensible soil and the urge to uproot as time goes by.

328.   Creek splashing in sulking storm mists.

329.   The hard truths of withered hands.

330.   The tuck and roll of river reeds at the bidding of a light breeze.

331.   The vanity of the moon to be awake on daylight's turf.

332.   The dustbowl age of the American frontier.

333.   Moments of deliberation in the seconds of a cigarette pull.

334.   A soothing, in the scent of fresh-cut bluegrass by the ethereal glow of day's eve.

335.   The soft poise of quaking aspen.

336.   Beach wood, bonfire-tall, on the rise toward the celestial ceiling.

337.   Shades of black and white, and the liberation of gray areas.

338.   The way pressed pages spring to life with each turn.

339.   The healing balm of baby chicks chattering.

340.   The unspoken discontent of women as mothers.

341. Ironing your wrinkled personality to fit in.

342. The flutter of city lights above taverns in the bad parts of town.

343. Missing pieces of a glass heart glued back together.

344. Being the paint to someone's monochrome canvas.

345. Choosing a skin suit for the day.

346. Twangy feedback from a country song slide guitar.

347. The toothpick grin and dusty heels of desperados.

348. Parallels between paradoxes and possibilities.

349. Drifters in blacktop mirages.

350. Wholesome tidings of weary wanderers emerging from rolling sandstorms.

351. The shimmer of your demons in opium smoke delusions.

352. Toasting the things that scare you most.

353. First drafts on tints of green you can't recall.

354. A state of ephemerality and sanguine smiles.

355. Dawdling in a daisy field daze.

356. Sensations of drowning in undertows.

357. Kodak keepsakes.

358. Secrets of sweeping seaweed.

359. Sprightly strolls beneath sashaying blues.

360. Corked greens of Sonoma Valley reds, and coastal air.

361.	Fusing and folding into your person.

362.	The reverence in heightened pulses.

363.	Bodies of copper-hot heat rubbing together.

364.	Chancing today by trusting tomorrow.

365.	Blanket retreats in grass lush and untamed.

366.	Loving and larking with wildflower beauties.

367.	Tinfoil skin that crinkles and reflects star flare.

368.	The feeling of leaf fibers and foxtails in your ankle socks.

369.	The way driveway spalling reminds you of your fading mother.

370.	Lamplight profiles and arching backs.

371.   A dew-trickle mountain floor morn.

372.   The foreshadowing of a fallen angel's salvation through servitude.

373.   The last of all the first best lines.

374.   Scrawling and scratching ink and blood on a poet's papyrus.

375.   Playing the chords that tell the stories of the weather where you're from.

376.   Indulging new dreams in place of old nightmares.

377.   Placing bent knees to pavement in prayer.

378.   The woeful eyes of wildlings watching over us.

379.   Blue blemishes of beryl woven with marbled whites overhead.

380.   Galaxies of goings-on, ongoing and going on behind the glazed gossamer.

381.   Slate-gray skies and indomitable chill.

382.   The orchard days of our mother's mothers.

383.   A dash of the devil in your grin.

384.   Dancing the midnight moods away.

385.   Something akin to a sensation.

386.   Rooftop lantern evenings with friends.

387.   Clothesline scented hand-me-downs.

388.   The wide swoop and loop in tying shoelaces.

389.   The crook of a broken nose.

390.   Gulls aflight against the ember-orange.

391.   Letting loose on wafer wings amidst the flaxen glow of mountain fields.

392.   Driving and sliding into b-side stories of being eighteen again.

393.   Fishing in the high ceiling of the galactic divide, where the astral arm of the ocean meets heaven.

394.   The way older women don't cry but dab away the wet.

395.   Plum blossom pinks of the Orient.

396.   Sewing your patchwork souls into the atmosphere.

397.   When the night is out during the day, skulking and stealing over the land.

398.   Stairwell musk-like swamp fog.

399.   Pissing away your pension.

400.   Moonlight serenading your window soul.

401.   Horse-drawn carriages and hot cocoa.

402.   Playground hierarchies.

403.   Tireless proponents of whim and desire.

404.   Standing tall against torrential rains.

405.   Shadows swaying rhythmically to flickering flames.

406.   Shallow blankets of sparkling blue.

407.   Heartlands of our ancestors.

408.   The explosive pull of a mighty cutthroat.

409.   Meandering streams giving way lazily to slumbering pools.

410.   The spectacle of a palatial mountain valley.

411.   A place where weeds and fescue can take root and run wild.

412.   The solemnity of swans on frosted ponds.

413.   A camaraderie between spilled drinks and stubbed toes.

414.   The randomness of coyote roadkill.

415.   Winds on wet skin.

416.   Hearts that glow in steam on bathroom mirrors.

417.   Firefly flashes of luminescence that hang in the air.

418.   The sound of barking sea lions from boardwalk banisters.

419.   Effervescent illumination bubbling and spilling over salted peaks.

420.   The eerie familiarity of ghost towns.

421.   The murmur of a babbling brook.

422.   New mother's smiles and the buzz of cafe conversations.

423.   Discarded furniture under freeway overpasses.

424.   Kids dancing to songs you listened to at their age.

425.   Winds wilder than Hell hound howls.

426.   Parables of poets who have pondered the cosmos.

427.   Bluegrass banjo bouquets.

428.   A space so infinite that God could hear his thoughts.

429.   Trading in your leisure for button-downs.

430.   The cold brick of alleyways and carousel sounds in the distance.

431. Asking a dying poet his thoughts on death.

432. The lack of silence in concrete.

433. Flannel and scruff and camper hair.

434. Poetry in pinecone dust.

435. Earthly verses chirped by woodland creature choruses.

436. Communing with river water.

437. Floating in a tallgrass cricket cadence.

438. The air of indifference between your father and his father.

439. Taking time to take time.

440. Rains that swell and bleed rich colors.

441. Giving away your desire for simplicity to ambition.

442. The fleeing of mosquitoes in dead-end towns.

443. The way old folks give the most colorful eulogies.

444. The soft squeeze of new palms.

445. Thumping along in the Bay Bridge brume.

446. Knowing the blessing of your father's able hands.

447. Pulsating to a vibrating sky.

448. Highway diner anecdotes.

449. The temperament of mothers and fathers.

450. The petrichor of fallen tears.

451.   Grayscale runes of Texas storm clouds.

452.   Paint splashes of lightning.

453.   A tang of rubber on hot asphalt.

454.   The bigness of life.

455.   Mortar shell mornings and napalm smoke sunsets.

456.   The true length of cast shadows contemplating their sorrows.

457.   Compositions of stone, smoothed in the subterfuge of time and tide.

458.   Reflections in refractions.

459.   Salon patron gossip and magazine gawking.

460.   Sailing oceans in cotton candy ships.

461.   The taste of fire as a topic of regular conversation.

462.   Redemption in Bible verse bends and curves.

463.   Sleeping off a stupor.

464.   Fragile like fractiles.

465.   Dialogue with dreadful things that slink and steal away to the unfathomable.

466.   The honest earmark of desolation.

467.   The cracked asphalt of a deserted desert road.

468.   The language of men of laboring hands.

469.   Park bench brooding.

470.   Spruce tree solitude and poet wisdom.

471.   A time before dust and sage were brothers.

472.   The blush of raspberry red lips.

473.   Chasing the fringed edges of tattered maps.

474.   Exhaling a low swell of smoke-swirled sighs.

475.   Running the backstreets in the black hours.

476.   Finding out your open eyes have never been so closed.

477.   Graybeard years and mothball memories.

478.   Weighing all your options at a four-way stop.

479.   The brushstroke bite of red-heat hate that makes us bitter.

480.   The shuddering of six a.m. on a Saturday.

481.   A place before the is of now.

482.   Missing the things that meant the most when you were young.

483.   Being nowhere you've been before again.

484.   The sun-cracked demeanor of the Sahara wilds.

485.   The magic of trees that once knew the sage hands of time.

486.   Ocean breeze merriment and the grace of a mother's kiss.

487.   Bone-tiring toil.

488.   Living big and lassoing lightning.

489.   Learning to live with hating yourself a little less.

490.   Ghouls that flee in the flickering of gas lamps.

491.   An oddity that shadows the ground as it settles down.

492.   The sum of how short-lived we are.

493.   Walking through low tides on beaches older than you are.

494.   The soak of a monsoon season spate.

495.   A steel-cold slab of introspection.

496.   Finger tap rapping on death's door.

497.   Beethoven baselines.

498.   Transients of discard and refuse.

499.   Absorbing the enigmatic wonderment of the narrative of the cosmos.

500.   An alarming crescendo of cawing.

501.	Crooking a squinted-eye aloft.

502.	The weight of spring burial wreaths.

503.	A collection of collectives and compiled concerns.

504.	Concentrated efforts to keep cluttered corners clean.

505.	To live for love, not to die for the thought.

506.	Being sick with grief in midnight novellas.

507.	Staring at blank-penned pages, hoping to write a good line.

508.	The babbled-bliss of chattering hearts.

509.	Rescuing shells and old railroad ties before they're lost to time and silt.

510.	Ambling aimlessly in a memory museum.

511. Pastels of peeling peach wallpaper.

512. Solidarity through solitude and friendships measured as a fraction.

513. A foothold against the current.

514. A willingness to shoot for the sun on waxed-wings.

515. Sharp as knife blade knicks—the cruelty of children.

516. Googly-eyes and brushing surfaces.

517. Keeping up with a groundhog day grind.

518. Mid-twirl in a daisy flower daydream.

519. Tottering leisurely toward a gradient grave.

520. An age before the sway of flesh and folly.

521.   Brick grit of a skyscraper rooftop ledge.

522.   Deafening decibels of whirl winds.

523.   The Elms of old.

524.   Soils of prospect and promise.

525.   Hoisting the earth to please the moon.

526.   Kite-skied pleasantries.

527.   A tomorrowless today.

528.   The small quiver of waning wax.

529.   Swearing on something sacred.

530.   Dying to die.

531.   Something like a stack of Plath.

532.   Beautiful as a storybook garden goodnight.

533.   Hearts that beat big as Gods' bowling with boulders.

534.   Reverence in the bygones of black and whites.

535.   The safety of sand silting silently into the sea.

536.   Wondering while you wander.

537.   Sparked-hearts and eye contact in a lover's longing.

538.   Twirling a raindrop dust dance.

539.   Talk of trembling torso entanglement in rise-and-fall rhythms

540.   Clutched-hand communication and soul-stirring chatter.

541.   Plucking a lash and making a wish.

542.   Mad as mammals when we lust.

543.   The infinite possibilities of intimacy in its infancy.

544.   Sundresses and suspenders and wild grass love-making.

545.   Kisses to the wind, homeward to blushing cheeks.

546.   Desert storm love affairs.

547.   Slow-motion sunset on a cosmic backdrop.

548.   Pitter-patter planetary paint drip.

549.   Skin-to-skin stimulation and lip-locked lusting.

550.   The scrap and scatter where the butt end won't burn.

551. A winter, cold as a bone chill and twice as cruel.

552. Clattering wind chimes on farmhouse porticos.

553. Kind as a cherry blossom sunrise.

554. Country boy charm.

555. Getting around to getting around.

556. The sun, same as it ever was.

557. Rocking chair reminiscing.

558. Afghan afternoons.

559. Seasons of clover fields.

560. Unspoken slights between motherless fathers and the wives they resent.

561.   Reveling contentedly in madness.

562.   Being human and fostering humanity.

563.   An all-consuming world folding into itself.

564.   Backpack memories through places unknown.

565.   Secondhand solutions to first world follies.

566.   8-tracks you hum along to on the long haul.

567.   Reminders in rear-views.

568.   Your skin and bones and heart in transitive prose.

569.   Crying and consoling your karma behind closeted-doors.

570.   Between the fuzz of weekday benders.

571. Making amends for becoming your father.

572. Laughing when you're drunk and being somber when you're sober.

573. Selling your soul to the Devil at midnight crossroads.

574. The long echo of the tolling bells.

575. Boozing beautiful women with bad habits.

576. Putting on your Sunday best to beat the Monday madness.

577. Another rotation in a fishbowl existence.

578. Taking time to muse in sand and stone.

579. The melancholia in the reddening of autumn's leaves.

580. Summers' squandered in reckless youth.

581. The despair in naked lands of winter's ire.

582. Abandoning innocence for amusement.

583. Wondering about people, the coming and going.

584. Pictures and parcels of poems from life on the road.

585. All the unanswered amens.

586. Snow-hidden hibiscus asleep in spring-lingered slumber.

587. Sacrifice, the hard kind you can't walk away from.

588. Wind and snow conspiring against the sun just beyond your door.

589. A scream into the deafening void.

590. Whatever it could have been, it was.

591.   A courtesy to 1985 and the last year of true love.

592.   A few friends, the wilting flower types with words for bones.

593.   Scattering your ashes in winds of sonnets and psalms.

594.   Travelers, tramps called to nowhere.

595.   Where Sugar Pines shake hands with the clouds.

596.   The brush of ocean salt in your hair.

597.   The search for release in simple things.

598.   A wink and a wave from the back end of a boxcar.

599.   Aurora glisten, stretching from east to west.

600.   A fusion of skin and sweat in thrash and thrum.

601.   Misplaced love, found again in the moments before the sun's cresting.

602.   A "take care" type of goodbye.

603.   Pleading eyes and pursed lips too shy to say please.

604.   Incessant floorboards that refuse to settle.

605.   Sentences, sugar-sweet that drip a candy glaze right off the page.

606.   A steadied pen to write away all your sins.

607.   Rims of white wines lipped red.

608.   Peppered-glass on cheap linoleum.

609.   Echos of Oak and fist and irritability over the in-laws.

610.   The little things you won't remember in a mid-morning grog.

611.	Faith in rain, a cleansing thing.

612.	A pinch of blood, and Mary, and a dash of the good
	Dr.'s bootlegged bourbon.

613.	Pellets of crystalline crashing down outside your window.

614.	Sticky hardtops and stitches: battered brow lines from bad falls.

615.	Bones and ache and jaded skin.

616.	Remorse, alive and well in song lyrics and certain film scenes.

617.	Somewhere between reluctant eyes and restlessness.

618.	Babbling in the shaded hours about a poetess.

619.	Wandering the neon haze of abandoned city streets.

620.	Jumping, bone naked and without inhibition, into the blue beyond.

621. Stripping off your society skin.

622. The wide wonder of coral gardens.

623. A warmth and grace, post-coital embrace.

624. Magenta splashes against an ashen silhouette.

625. The piercing static of charred grays.

626. A symphony of extraordinary hues.

627. Meadows where silence muses peacefully.

628. A rhythm known only to the universe.

629. Dancing reckless the guilty pleasures of your heart.

630. The wisdom of stars abroad.

631. Stealing a kiss from a stranger.

632. Being alive in your life.

633. Cemetery fields of green.

634. Balding, bulging, and gas prices.

635. Going 120 in a car that can't handle the curves.

636. Knowing the favor of the universe.

637. Casting a string of love lines into cerulean tides.

638. The fancy of wandering heart clouds.

639. Mandolin grass lullabies.

640. Slighted fingers trembling at the temptation of touching.

641.   Traces of coveting in the swirl of milky residue.

642.   Wisps of mountain breeze.

643.   A quilt of love notes never sent.

644.   Adventures in stick sword shenanigans.

645.   Sketchbook shadings of serendipity.

646.   Desert campfire intercourse.

647.   Cola lips, sugar-sweet, and cherry red.

648.   Paradise in palpitations of pulsing hearts.

649.   Midnight's dawn in wasteland dreams.

650.   Mess and sex and countertop encounters.

651. Pub side busking for bread and wine.

652. Kissing collisions of astral fields.

653. Rafter beams that swell and sob.

654. Beneath the sway of kaleidoscoping-skies.

655. Coffeehouse courtships.

656. Moons that long for the low baying of wayward wolves.

657. Sacred things said in the savor of your lover's favor.

658. The space between the lines where rainstorm reveries take place and kisses spark electric.

659. The positive power of negative hands on crushed napes.

660. Soft exhales lost to impassioned waters.

661.   80 degrees in the dead of winter.

662.   Bills and debt and death and dirt.

663.   Breathing sex breath in the still of night.

664.   The dull burnout of a chalky haze.

665.   Sparse leaves dangling noncommittally.

666.   The ignorance of one-horse towns.

667.   Jeering pigs advocating for idiocracy.

668.   Being drunk on crap beer, dancing to country whoop.

669.   Privilege and posh neighborhoods.

670.   Scripted moaning and orchestrated orgasms.

671. The way disappointed mothers look at their sons.

672. A vehicle that isn't worth the payment.

673. The tingle of fingers tickling the spine.

674. Chemtrails from winter inversion.

675. The dangers of neglectful consumerism.

676. Snow that sounds like a cocked gun.

677. Something boozenly poetic.

678. Listening to songs that meant something once.

679. Whistling sounds that blow through abandoned trailers.

680. Mountains with a demeanor.

681.   The divisiveness of social media.

682.   The comings and goings of latchkey kids.

683.   The crash and burn of first kisses.

684.   How the stars look in moonless canyons.

685.   Ink waves on paper oceans.

686.   Caring for something you don't care about.

687.   Summer scorch and magnifying glasses.

688.   Falling out of moving cars.

689.   Questions that are better left unanswered.

690.   Discarded cigarettes in sidewalk cracks.

691. Atonement for loving washed away in the reverie of hearted exhales.

692. The moted-particles of a cracked barn door summer's eve sunlight.

693. Walking in tones of sepia overlay.

694. The tragedy of caged-heart companions.

695. Scribbling red the skylines of the world.

696. The sweet sounds of wide-open plains.

697. Lines and strokes canyon-deep that are breathtaking to behold.

698. Promises of passage to passion.

699. Writing love songs to the flutter-thump pounding of racing hearts.

700. The small hours of bated breathing.

701.   The treasures waning moons impart to the bold.

702.   Passion waves that bid sink or swim.

703.   Longing to long for idol eyes.

704.   The space between ripples.

705.   The torment of never knowing your father's heart.

706.   Cross-legged and cradled in sweltered-skin.

707.   Curious hands.

708.   The beg and brace for sweet relief.

709.   Covenants made in confidence.

710.   An ache to be drunkenly delighted in affection.

711.   The siren call of fervency.

712.   Sinking into folds of velveteen.

713.   The disheartening of hardened hearts.

714.   The scents of autumn air in the infinity of marshes wild.

715.   Feeling a heartbeat skip a thousand miles away.

716.   Borders and boundaries between state line spirits.

717.   Smiles in frames of dusking-glow.

718.   Fishing pull tugs and walks in Douglas fir.

719.   Breaking the monotony with boudoir biology.

720.   Entwined in eager evening embrace.

721. Pursuits in wild abandon.

722. Muddy banks where cattail cotton spread their stories far and wide.

723. Thundering renditions of "Moonlight Sonata."

724. Swatting cloud wisps on mountains high.

725. The heavy mind of the seers.

726. Waiting on a ballon sky to pop.

727. Heel-clack echos.

728. Running against the grain and swimming upstream.

729. Boiled and brimming emotions that run hot and flow over.

730. The spark that sours and salts your mouth with hate.

731.   An elevator existence in ups and downs.

732.   Tree swing days long forgotten.

733.   Peaks lightly seasoned with a dash of white.

734.   Where red ferns grow and wild things are.

735.   Brushstrokes of clarity in insanity.

736.   Waterlogged tributes to tears and torment.

737.   The triumph of worlds transcended by the power of thoughts.

738.   Confetti dust dancing.

739.   The ticka-tocka tempo of splashed puddles.

740.   A slow drip into sedated slumber.

741. Perpetual hurtling through stages of change.

742. The cross that migrant mothers bear.

743. Apathetic inclinations.

744. The generosity of drifters.

745. Identities lost to change and age.

746. Obedient cogs in a greater apparatus.

747. Afflictions that know no clemency.

748. The vibrations of boisterous laughter.

749. Finding a haven in observation.

750. Polaroid printouts and merry-go-round merriment.

751. The truth of mortality in cloud dissipation.

752. The weighted glance of rear-view mirror eyes.

753. Shifted-hip propositions.

754. Mindless conversation between reality TV commercials.

755. Punching with kisses.

756. The definitive sounds of closed coffins.

757. Where dreamers unfurl their harp string wings.

758. Gliding idly through star currents.

759. How shadows speak soundlessly your secrets with other shadows.

760. Tobacco pipe tales of dusted coffee can coin collections.

761.   The calming of commas.

762.   Breaking to banquet in wine and cheese picnic blankets.

763.   Hydrangea hues.

764.   History rooted in the swell of whipped dust.

765.   Hell or high water come and gone.

766.   Words that resound in deafening torment.

767.   A complete and total catharsis of the existential mentality.

768.   The winters old folks speak of.

769.   Finger curled hair.

770.   A child with child and bigger dreams of better things.

771. Sleeping better knowing tomorrow's problems from tonight will still be the same as yesterday's.

772. The calculus in facial cracks.

773. Thinking on the surety of stars blinking out for good.

774. The contentment of cracked leather in vacated vehicles.

775. The boredom of boardwalks in a June gloom burn-off.

776. Collecting cold cash to compensate the ferryman.

777. 2 a.m. fixations.

778. The oppression of hymnal history.

779. Parades of ponderosa.

780. Duking things out with dashboard hands.

781.   A song, lyrics unsung, on a soundtrack to your life.

782.   Where violence and vitriol collide in a cavalcade of nuance.

783.   A rumbling of hooves.

784.   Crabs clawing at the sides of a bucket, pawing and pulling at each other's best attempts to be free.

785.   Running behind outrunning the horizon.

786.   Soaring free above the white noise.

787.   The cool of evening's blush.

788.   The ember scribblings of a midday sun's erratic musings.

789.   Trading in good looks for a silver tongue.

790.   Portraits of hardened men on horseback.

791. Laughter in silent films.

792. A craving for pre-dawn woods.

793. Discovering yourself anew in your child's laughter.

794. A moment of truth to salve or shatter all hope.

795. Waves of silken sheet.

796. A sweet spot, surrounded by cotton tuft and tree petal budding.

797. Hearkening the siren song of your inner hedonist.

798. A restiveness that reaches fever pitch levels left unchecked.

799. Wading through warm lips.

800. Touches that keep their commitments.

801. The things tender lovers won't tell you.

802. Stories from the margins.

803. The two of you as ampersands.

804. Christmas whiteout nostalgia.

805. Tobacco incense and photo poems.

806. Smudges of melancholy.

807. Homemade soup and soda bread.

808. A quarter past your darkest hour.

809. Second-hand bookstore flirtations.

810. Tripping into rabbit holes.

811.   Solitude and a cuppa Turkish.

812.   The fine art of swooning.

813.   Epicurean thresholds.

814.   Towering shrines to womanhood.

815.   Scrubbing someone's meaning from your teeth.

816.   The unsatisfied ache of Narcissus.

817.   The consolation of a slow news day.

818.   A hush in the humdrum.

819.   Cloaked evil in random kindness.

820.   Streetlamp fizzle and wine slogging.

821. Urban murals of white linen lines.

822. A tempered gaze into the edge of everything.

823. Larking in the American dream.

824. The clumsy choruses of cathedral bells.

825. Fence lengths of farmyards.

826. Buttered milieu and a pot of worldliness.

827. The press and rub of corduroy during church sermons.

828. Austerity in folded blankets.

829. The cutlery of menacing metaphors.

830. A golden pint or three in musking-dives.

831.   The phobia of sagging dermis getting under your skin.

832.   The span of eternity in cross-country soundtracks.

833.   Lace-felted slips and naughty fingertips.

834.   The endlessness of evergreens.

835.   Constructs to measure relativity.

836.   Profiles of antique turquoise.

837.   Parents who know better but forget themselves.

838.   Complex conversations with Madness.

839.   The rainbow history of the cosmos.

840.   Lifetimes in blinking.

841. The inhuman howlings of English Moors.

842. Window faces from the backseat of departing cars.

843. Air guitar symphonies.

844. Indulging in odors of pine-fir perfume.

845. Where aging oaks splinter and split.

846. Buying yourself an opinion with your last two sense.

847. Before being too old to know better, and telling yourself you won't become like those before you.

848. Elevated eyebrows and shattered windshields.

849. The way people never smiled in photos from the outlaw days.

850. The drum of capable horses behind your gas pedal.

851.   A coveting of ferry tern monogamy.

852.   The fearlessness of seasons in the shadow of the reaper.

853.   An oath to write off the injustice of mirrors.

854.   Stockpiles of notepad failures.

855.   Concept art of a watercolor Arcadia.

856.   The chaos of naked feet on cold linoleum.

857.   The gossip of creatures unseen.

858.   Clusters of porch light gnats.

859.   Schoolyard fisticuffs and bully besting.

860.   Habitual rituals.

861. Whiplash from stairway ghosts.

862. The lurk of hummingbird wing hallucinations.

863. The composure of amphitheater reverberation.

864. Sweating out your penance in L.A. bathhouses.

865. Pyre heaps of Viking bones.

866. The stink of single malt abuse in rundown tenements.

867. The aesthetic of ultra-violence.

868. The inconsiderate drift of burned-out satellites.

869. Rendered negatives of pier water.

870. The way misery loves materialism.

871. The subtlety of nipple-pink.

872. Chateaux getaways on the Périgord.

873. Poking at refrigerator garbage in a daytime doldrum.

874. Silhouettes of tented-pines along the Blackfoot of Missoula.

875. The blood rush sensation in kisses we crave.

876. A dream of dreams collapsing, crimping, and creasing from the corners.

877. Venues where the possessed lie awake and obsess the little things.

878. Tired and tiresome, tiring of the pollen, sick of sneezing, and bored of the baloney.

879. The steep currency of cheap backtalk.

880. The damnable stale of sobriety.

881.   Ambiguous acknowledgments.

882.   Stagnate bathwater and waxing philosophical.

883.   Taking umbrage with a swamp witch.

884.   A prosetic waltz on the graves of proper grammar and syntax.

885.   Plain eggs and one-night stands for breakfast.

886.   Outrageous accusations of being happy and normal.

887.   The tickle of vinyl scratch.

888.   Arguments in voices like linted dryer vents.

889.   Champagne olive branches.

890.   Keeping your challenges from your children.

891. Hand-harvested oysters from the Flaggy Shores.

892. Prophets in empty shot glasses.

893. Heedless leisure through unspoiled glimmer.

894. Conch horn headaches.

895. The autonomy of anonymous note giving.

896. The infallibility that pigeons will never be regarded.

897. Submerging into New Year's Eve bath floors.

898. Saying yes, but meaning no.

899. Aqua spray from waved-hellos of whales off Alaskan coasts.

900. The general consistency of magazines in tattoo parlors.

901.   Scholarly debates over the existence of Valentinus.

902.   The aura and awe of floating trash seas.

903.   The piquant waff of cookie tins.

904.   The scandal of exposed shoulders in church halls.

905.   Questioning glances through the looking glass of smooth versus traditional jazz.

906.   The audacity of retro SciFi art.

907.   All the talk of turning back the doomsday clock.

908.   The hysteria of Ellis Island immigrants.

909.   The bizarre reality of burial businesses.

910.   The perfunctory nature of windmills in Amsterdam.

911.   The hypocrisy in gold-plated spires.

912.   The absurdity of yearning.

913.   Dreading the transaction of death, and not the finality of it.

914.   Ticket stubs from tourist attractions within your life.

915.   Rebar fingers peeling back concrete skin.

916.   Ghosts at the Russian roulette table.

917.   Riptides of clock hand revolutions pulling you under.

918.   Godless Christian anecdotes.

919.   Insomnia as a cure for existentialism.

920.   Verbal emasculation from your predecessors.

921.   How nothing smarts like being stupid for love.

922.   Casio keyboard rockstar mollycoddling.

923.   Eggshell tiptoeing around asking.

924.   Urban street photography nuances.

925.   Chain link fence chitchat.

926.   Market loss masochism and the band-aid bull.

927.   Bleach blonde wigs and bachelorette parties.

928.   The generation of flat caps and boiler suits.

929.   Shelved notions of suicide.

930.   Rubbing last night's malt sting out of your eyes.

931.   Deviating from the ordinary.

932.   Couching off your bad ankles.

933.   The way stillness shivers at adultery.

934.   The misconception that justice is blind and not just blindfolded.

935.   Food stamp vouchers and the steady rise of grocery inflation.

936.   Dying poor because of your convictions.

937.   Longhand, in old English script.

938.   Dull labor and getting by.

939.   Bruised knee repentance.

940.   The harsh squabbling of startled geese.

941. The deep drowse of oblivion.

942. Sifting through an assortment of useless buttons.

943. Homeless shelter rhapsodies and the deaf ears of Congress.

944. Patience through the anger of the terminally ill.

945. Beaver dam deliberations.

946. The cuckolding of social justice.

947. Diesel truck fumigation and disregard for the ozone.

948. The dizzying effect of patterned-carpets in hotel hallways.

949. Medieval ruins on Scotland isles.

950. Mending your mental stonewalls.

951.   Subconsciousness that roams in a nightdress.

952.   How the coming is quicker than the going.

953.   Refusing flood insurance, then seeing your home swept downstream.

954.   Pushing around tomato slop and wondering where your life went.

955.   The minutia of washing dishes.

956.   Cinnamon roasted pecan stimulation.

957.   Cuddles with your snuggly creatures.

958.   The satire of beloved cutlery and crystal goblets.

959.   Porpoising through your purposelessness.

960.   The vacancy of soluble ends ashed into empty trays.

961. Salvation at the bottom of backyard swimming pools.

962. The dogmatic lauding of non-taxable denominations.

963. Recognizing people for who they are and not who you'd like them to be.

964. The immutable laws of feline paws.

965. The awkwardness of stallless bathrooms.

966. Feigned interest.

967. Mosaic swirls in the corridors of Raphael's Sistine sanctuary.

968. Regarding the anarchy of blizzards from behind aerating Earl Grey.

969. The parlor tricks of cautionary tales.

970. The roar of festering apartment building infernos.

971. Dangled toes in farmland tributaries.

972. Splashes of espresso on your Picasso morn.

973. The seemingly senseless flight patterns of butterflies.

974. Wearing your exhaustion as a cry for help.

975. The war paint faces of irises.

976. Victorian-era decadence in pencil sketch.

977. Roller queens and Juicy Fruit discothèques.

978. The humbling of hospice beds.

979. Jungian archetypes and complex disorders.

980. Reasonable aversions to daily routine.

981.   Marriage as an answer to boredom.

982.   Silent sobbing under warbling shower heads.

983.   The characteristic drawl of slouchers.

984.   Dank suburbs under waist-high laundry piles.

985.   The exhilaration of long shots and last chances.

986.   Bistro napkins with all of your best ideas on them.

987.   The steady hush of road-trippers passing bucolic junkyards.

988.   Proverbs that work out all your problems.

989.   The unsuspecting prickle of not being needed.

990.   Recounting your greatest calamities in time-lapse.

991.   The irony of making your bed and sleeping in it.

992.   The polarization of evolution.

993.   The cerumen polish of the recently deceased.

994.   The questionable air of lovable people.

995.   Understanding the noxious influence of animal's milk.

996.   Learning to sit comfortably for extended amounts of time.

997.   Bullet train relationships that wind down to a muttering of weather reports.

998.   The collective pause to mourn Notre-Dame.

999.   Tango sex and sexless tangos.

1000.   The glaring ideal dissimilarities between you and your siblings.

Acknowledgments

To my family, friends, and amazing followers, I must express eternal gratitude. Your tireless support lifts my spirits daily and continues to give me strength and inspiration in my endeavors and writing. I truly could not chase my dreams without your love. If my words have reached you in any way, please, kindly leave a review for this book. Your time and thoughts are important to me.

About the Author

A lover of words and the impact they create, Ty Gardner is a lifelong enthusiast of all forms of poetry and has written creatively from the time he was a child.

When he's not musing and waxing poetic, Ty can be found exploring the wonderment of his newfound home in Northwest Arkansas with his wife, two children, and their handsome rescue pup, Archer.

He is the author of *By Way of Words: A Micro Prose Journey Through the Elements That Mold Us*, *Bukowski Charm: Trash Fire Poetry to Warm the Soul*, *Wild Life: Musings of a Mad Poet*, *From the Watercolor Garden: Poems of Life and Love*, *Exercises in the Abstract: Poems With No Name*, *Sunsets Over Cityscapes: Poems for the Existential Uprising*, *Papercut: A Chap-style Book of Prose*, and *Average American: Poems On Becoming Normal*. Some of his works can also be found in *VSS365 Anthology: Volume One*, released in September 2019.

Printed in Great Britain
by Amazon